# Daffodil

# A Photo Essay

# by

# Stephen M Kraemer

# Spring

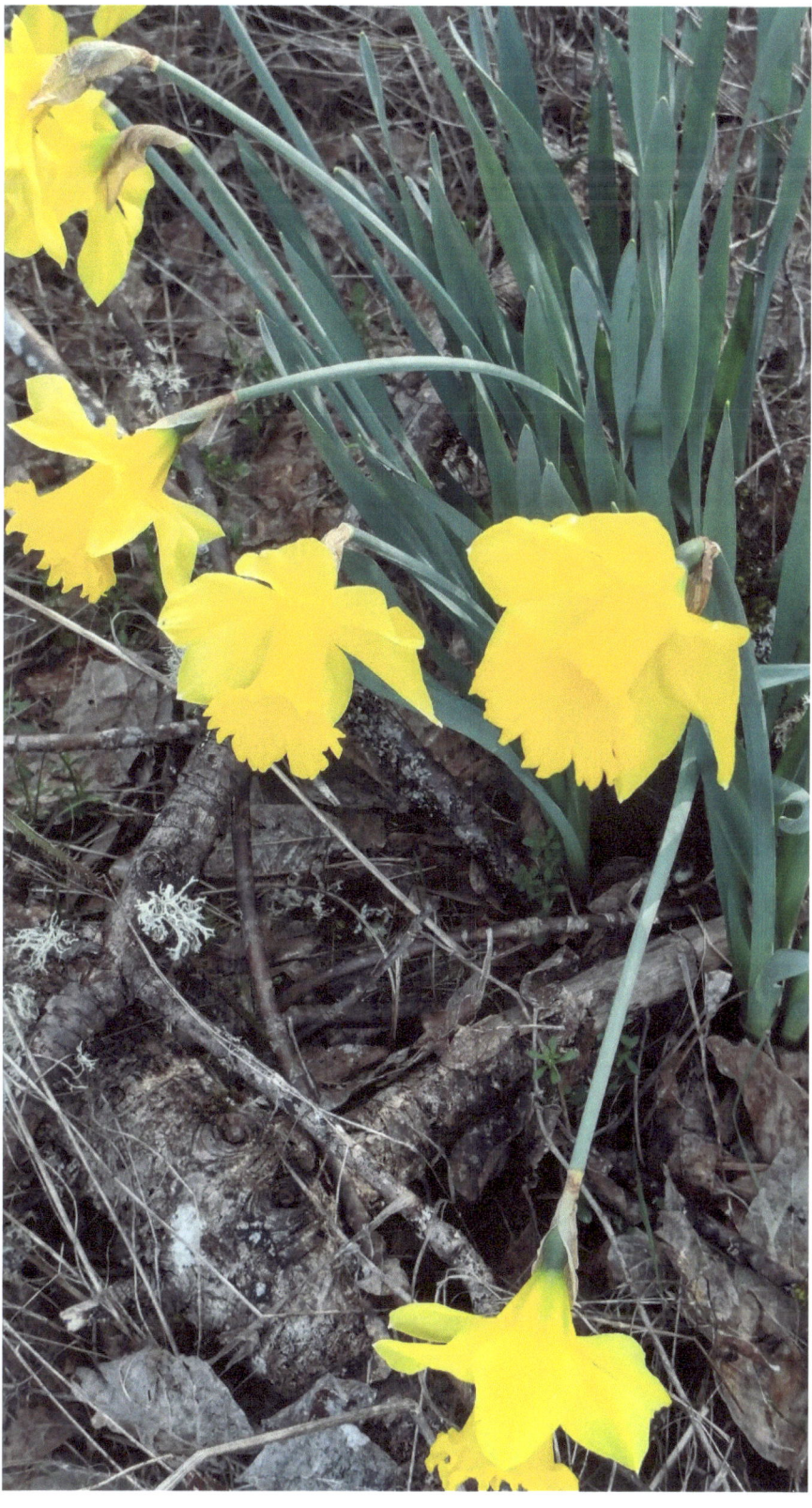

# Garden

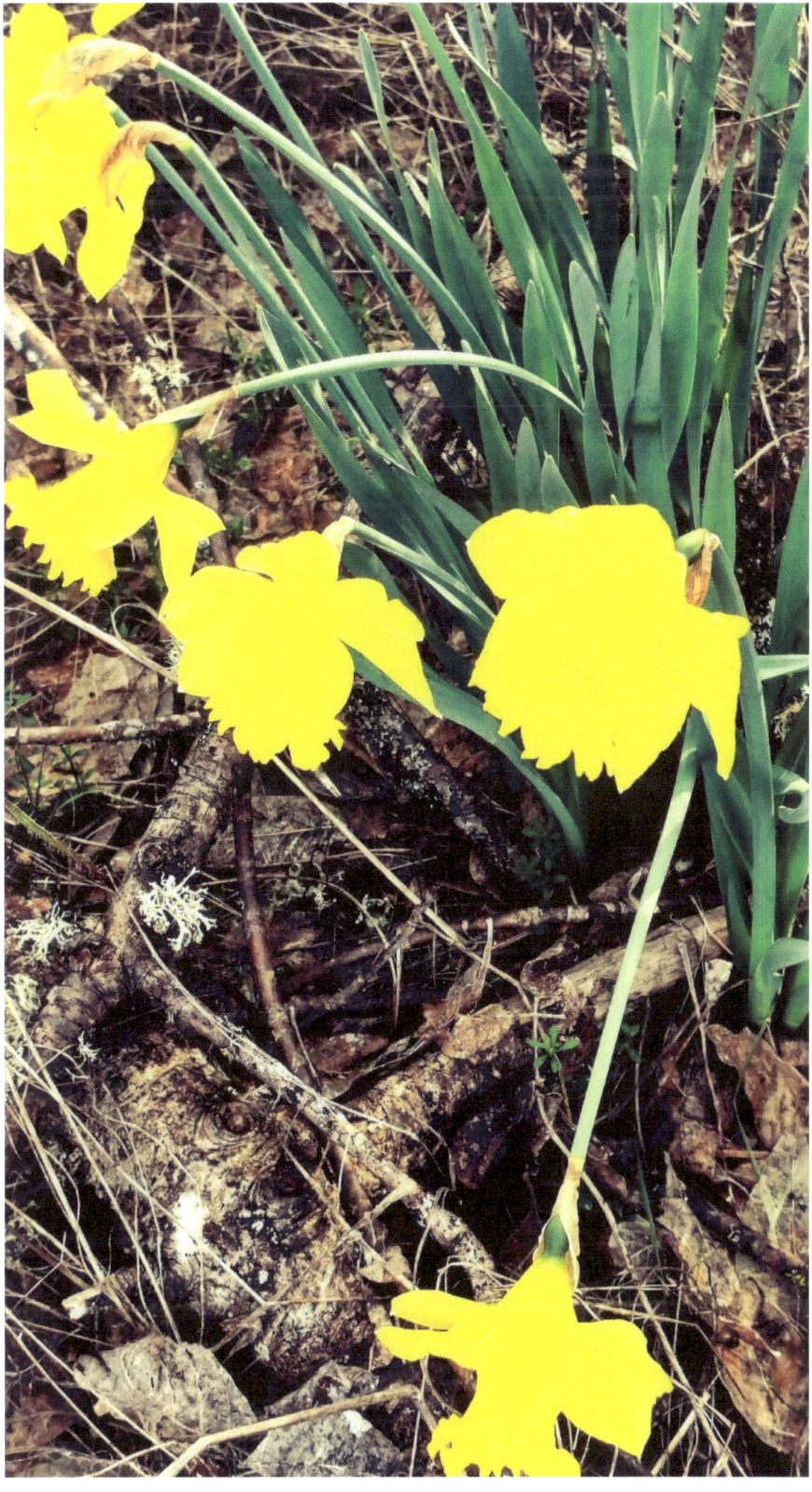

# Green

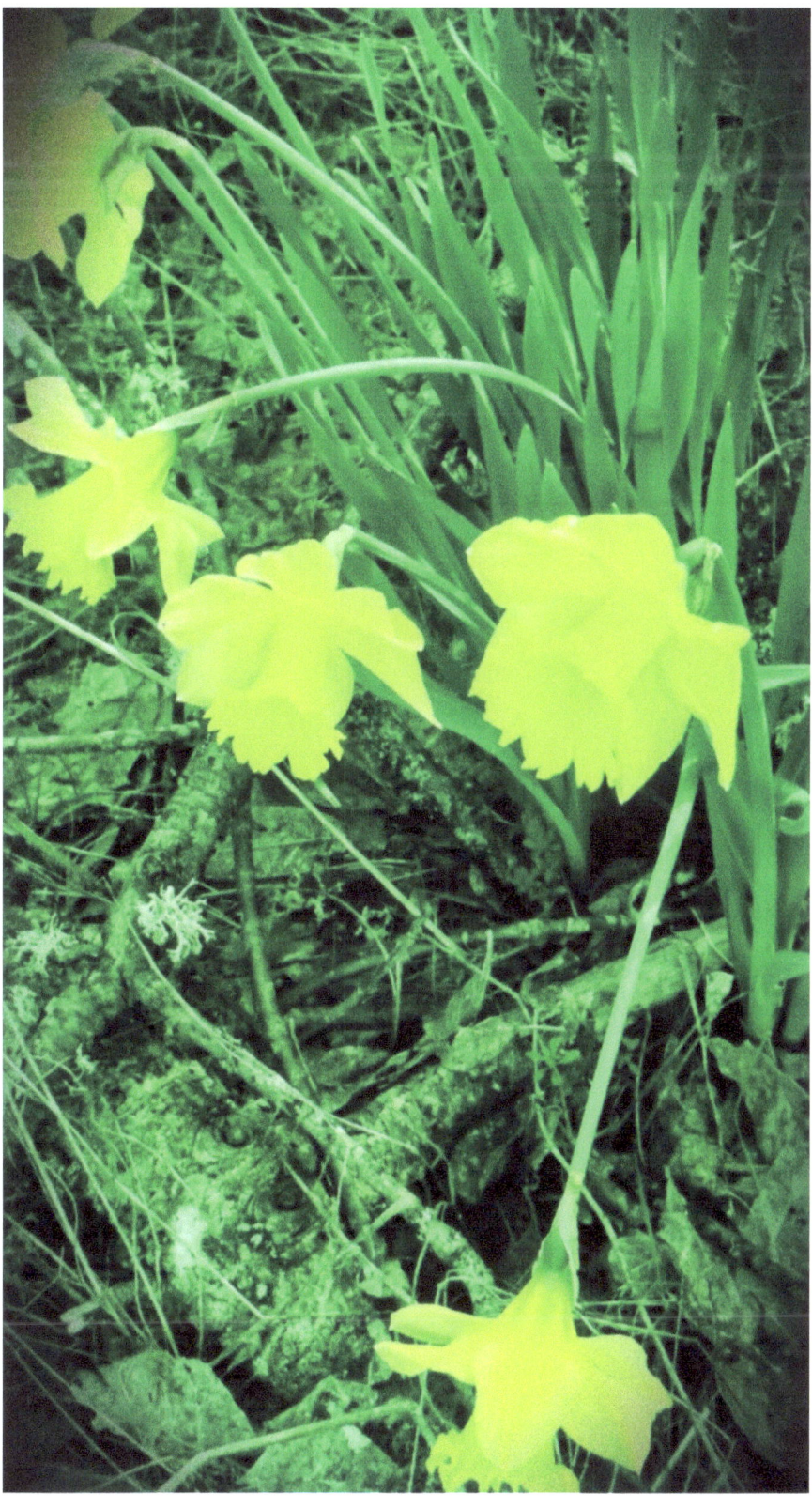

# New Beginnings

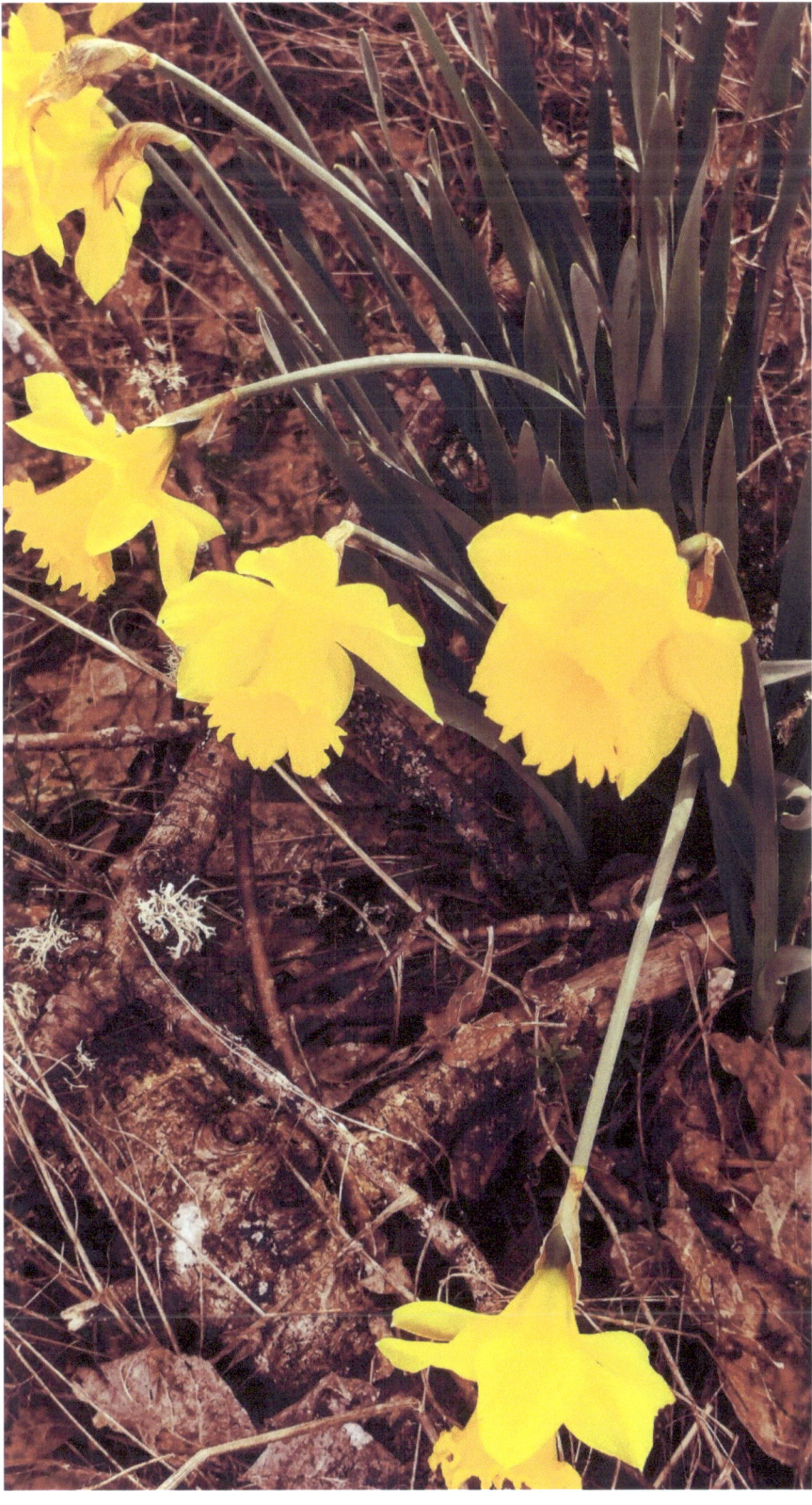

# Blue

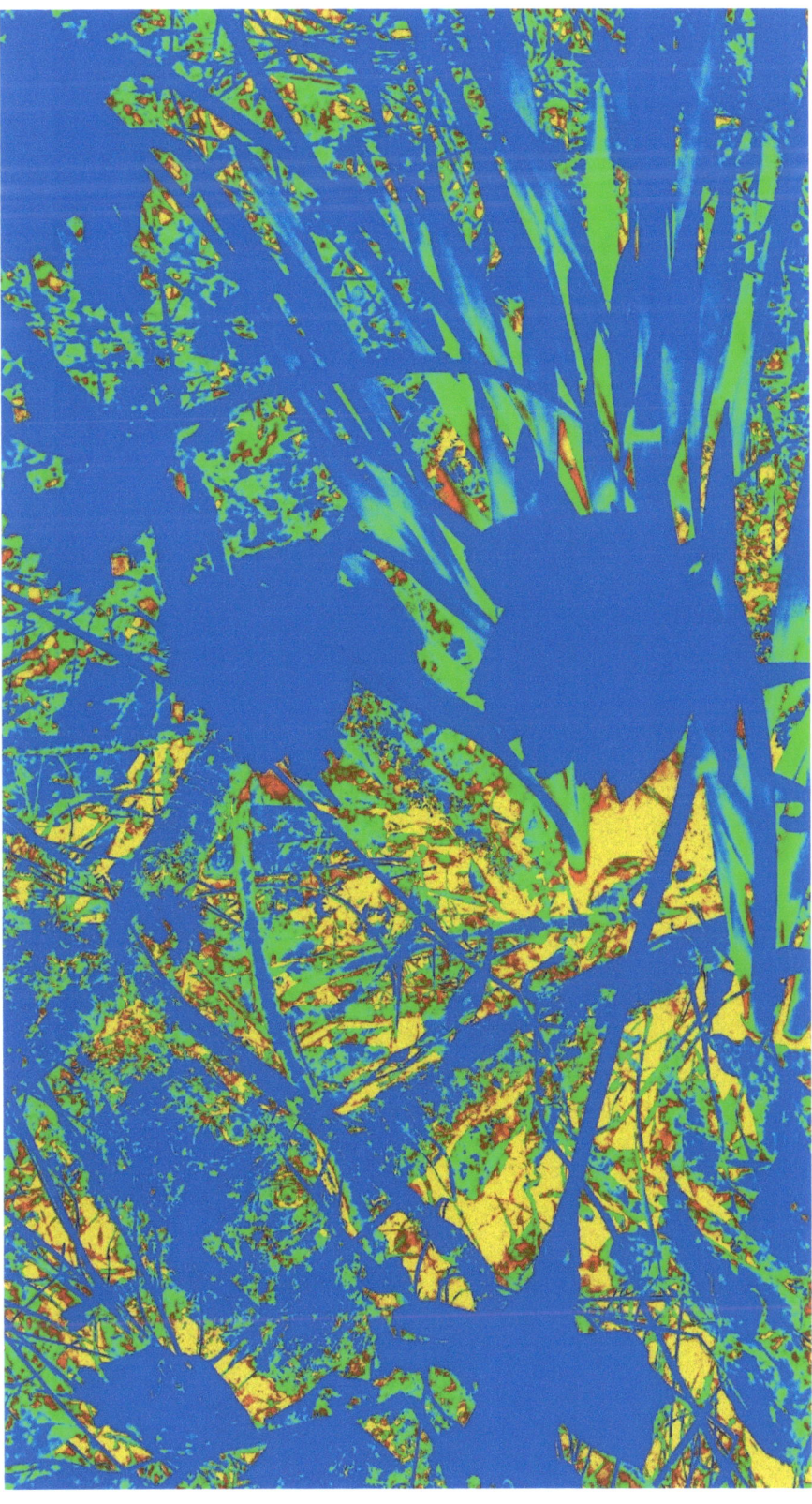

# Mixtures

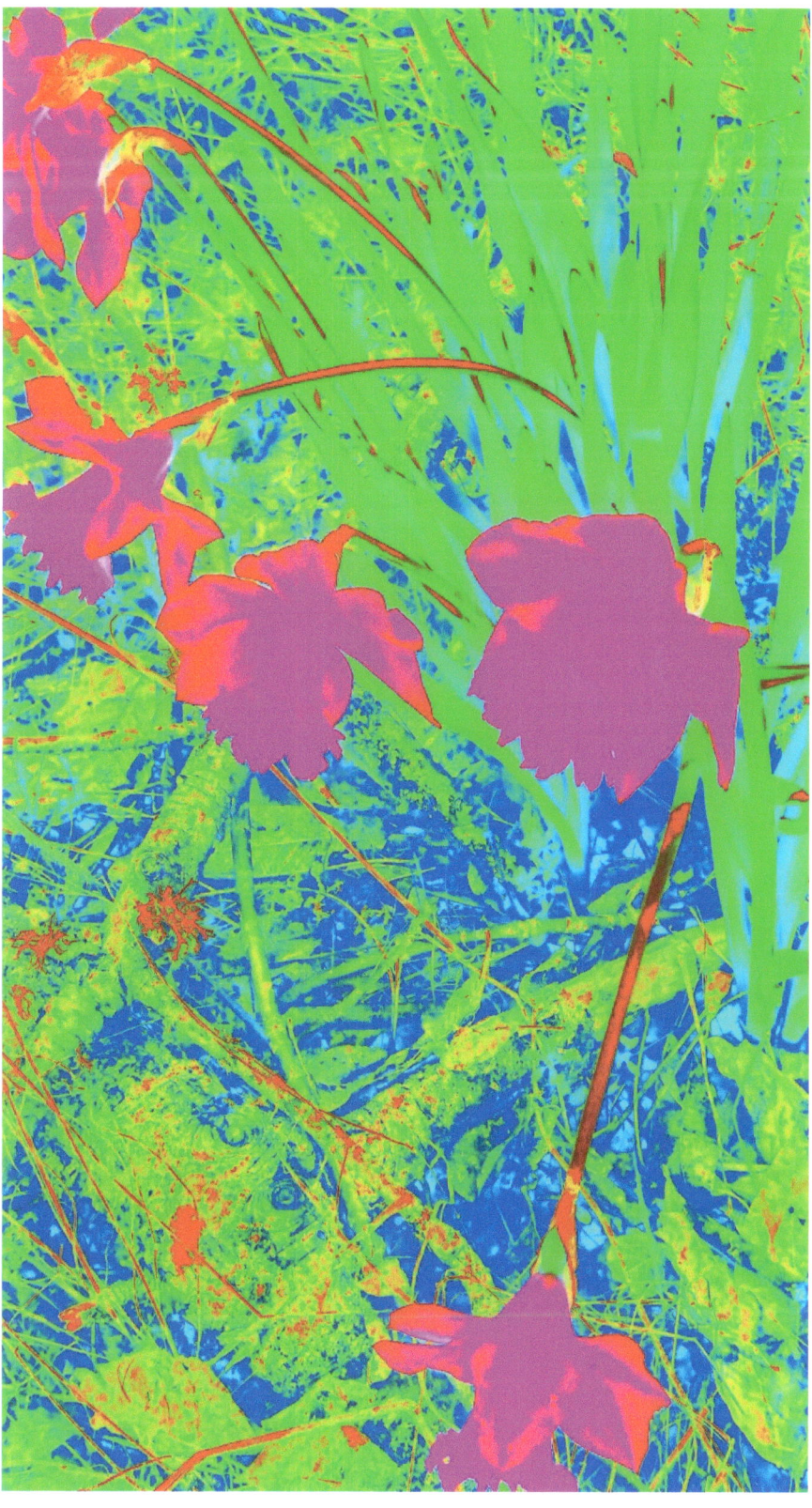

# Fire

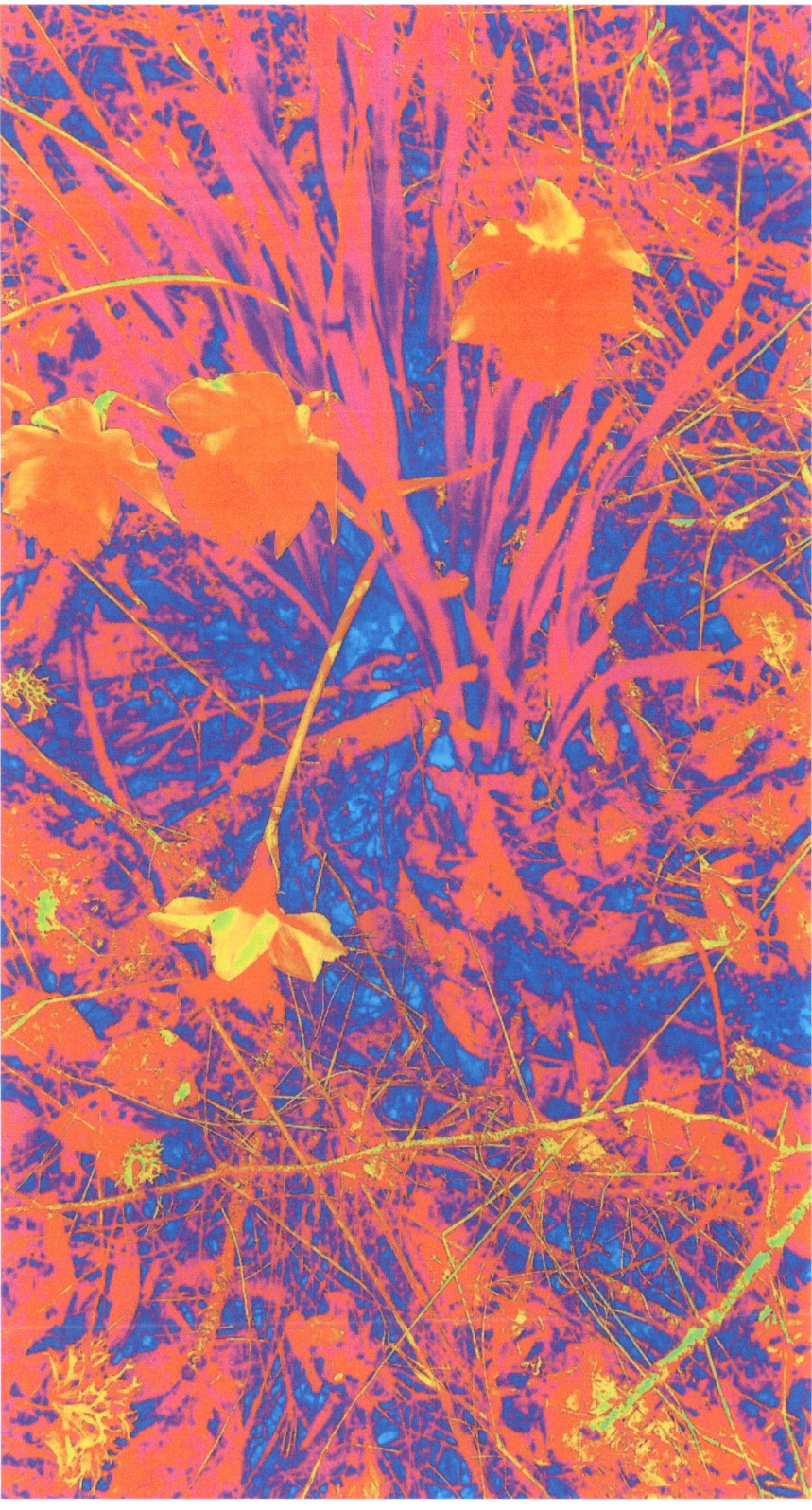

# Cool Blue

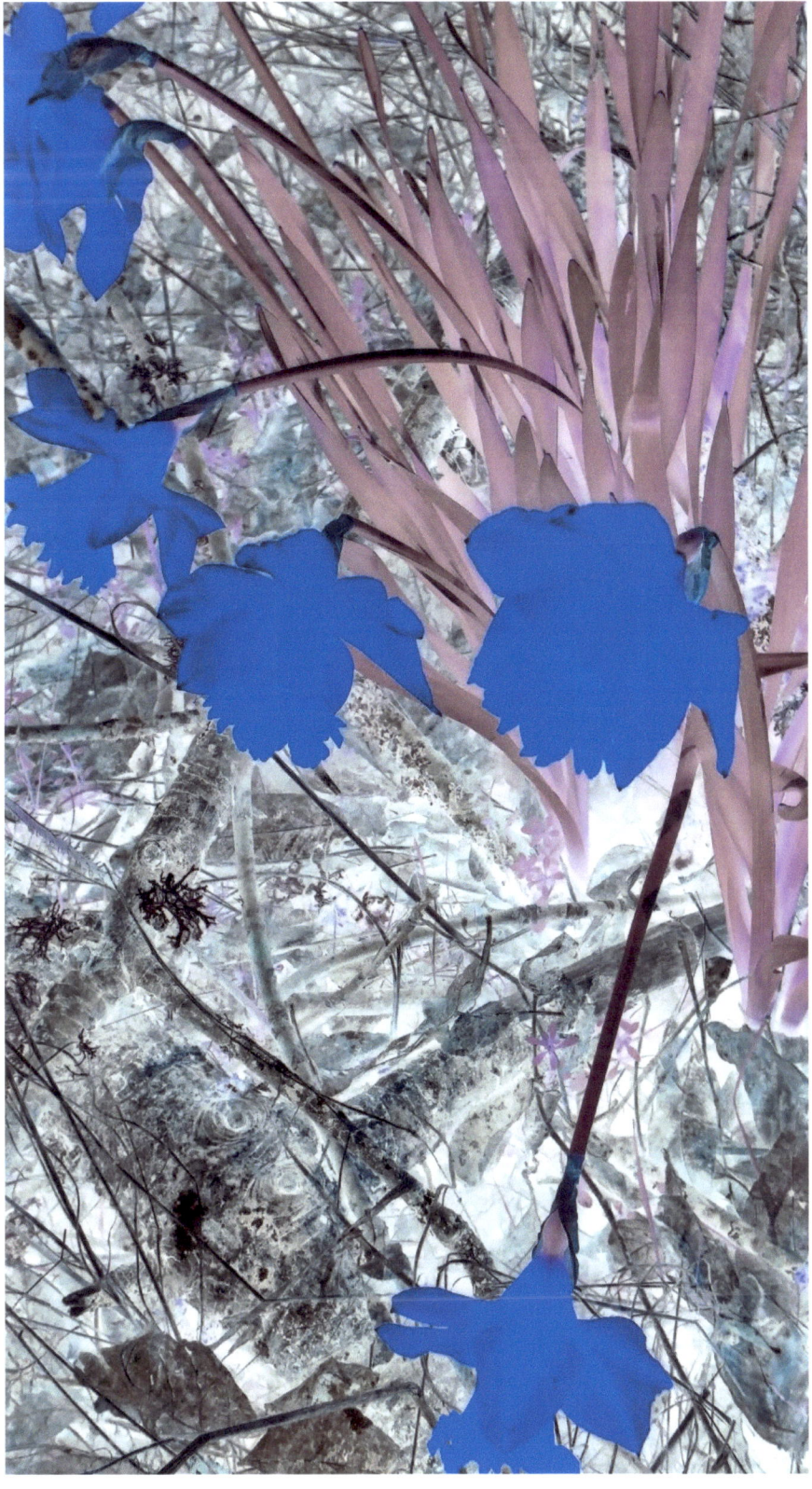

# Fantasies

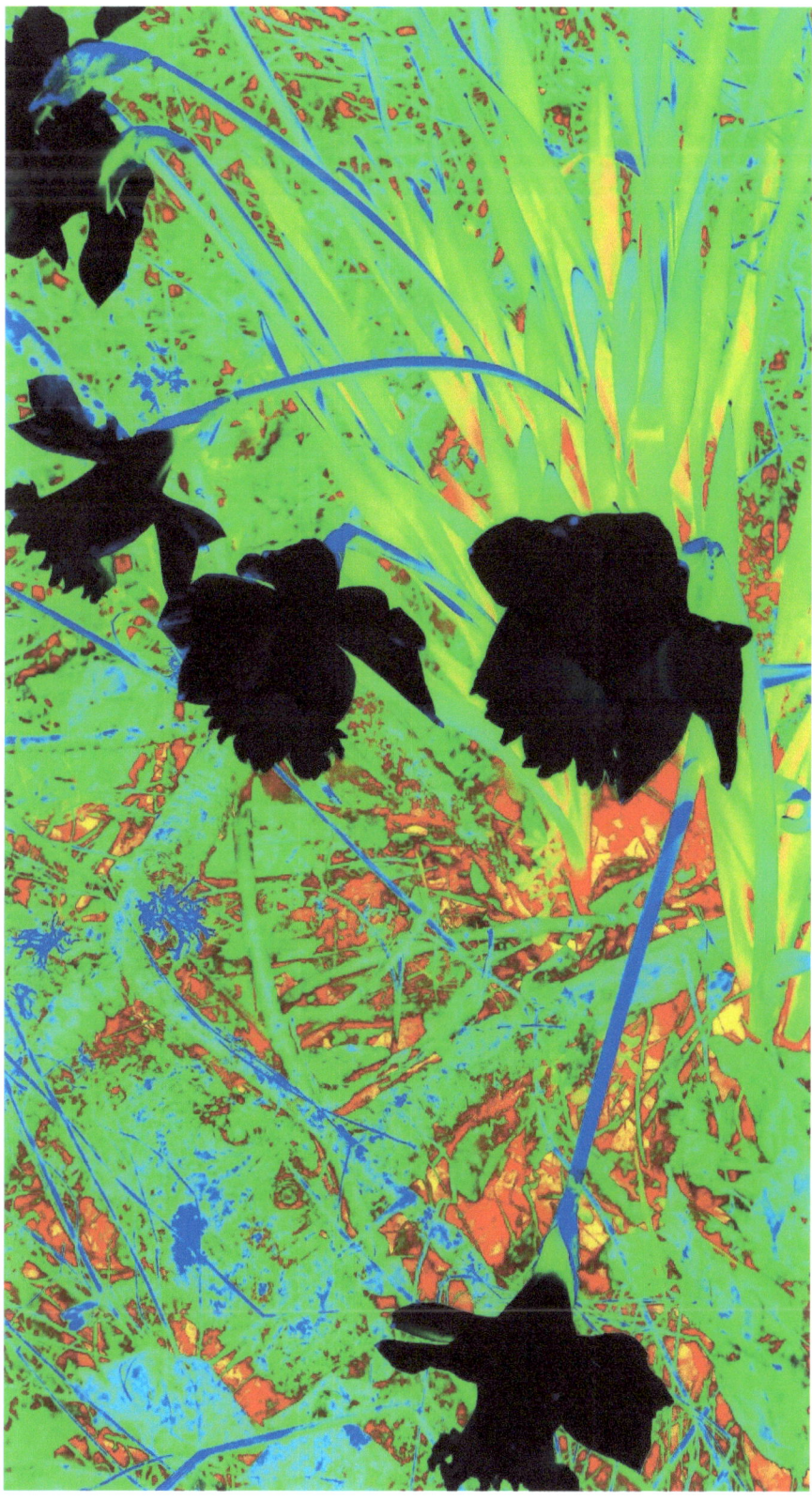

# Pinks

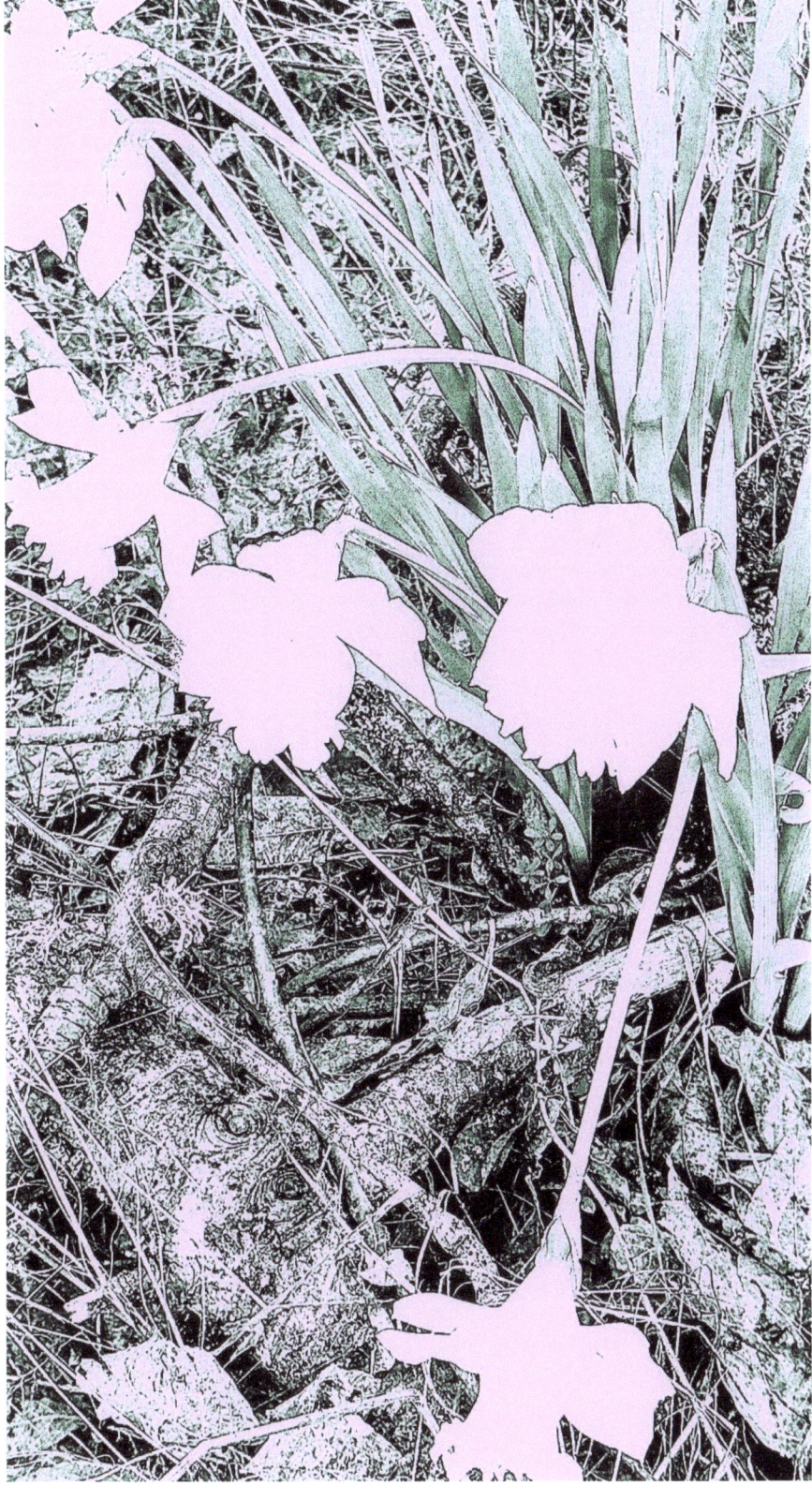

# Mild Climate

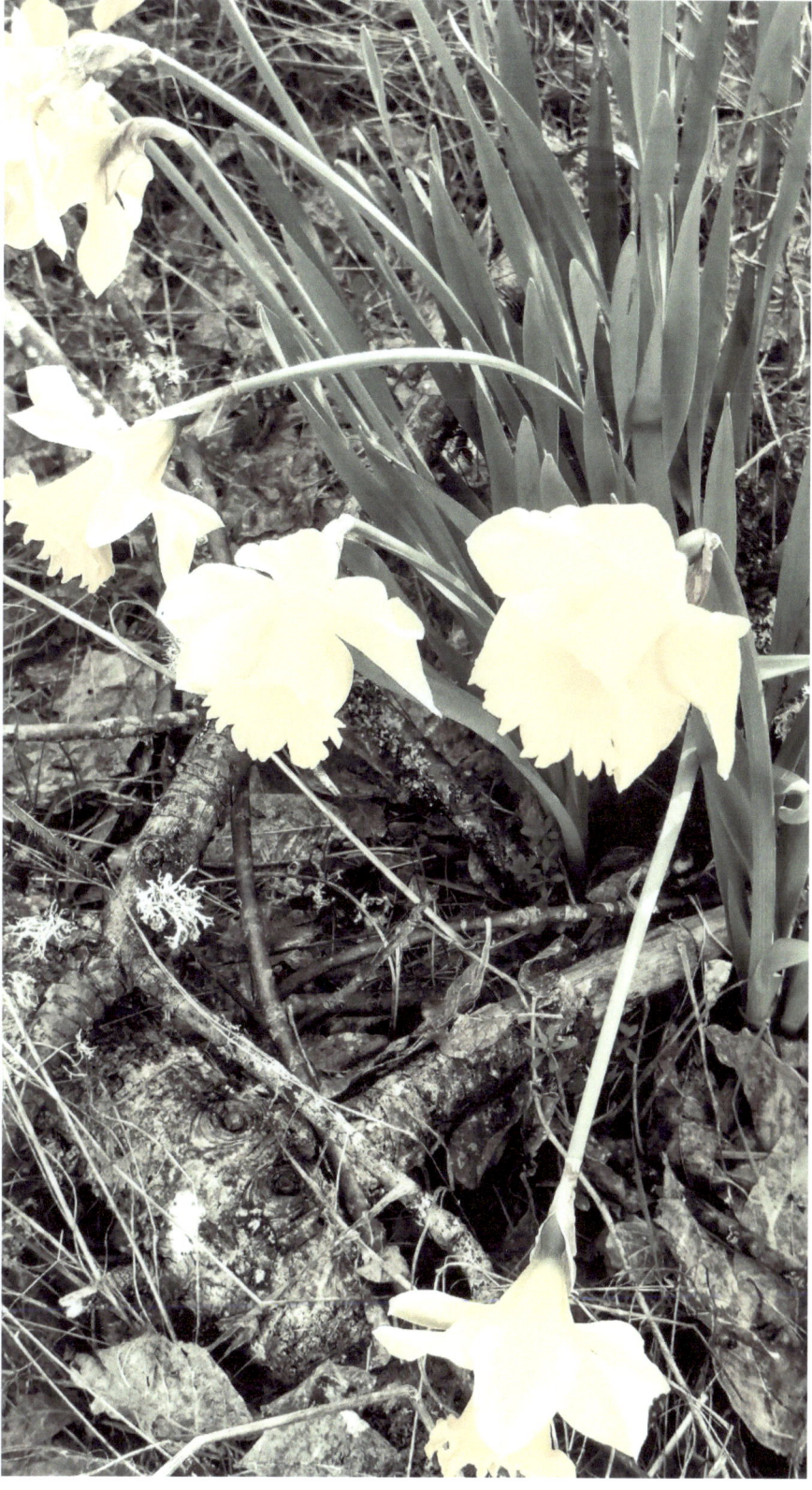

# Ocean Breeze

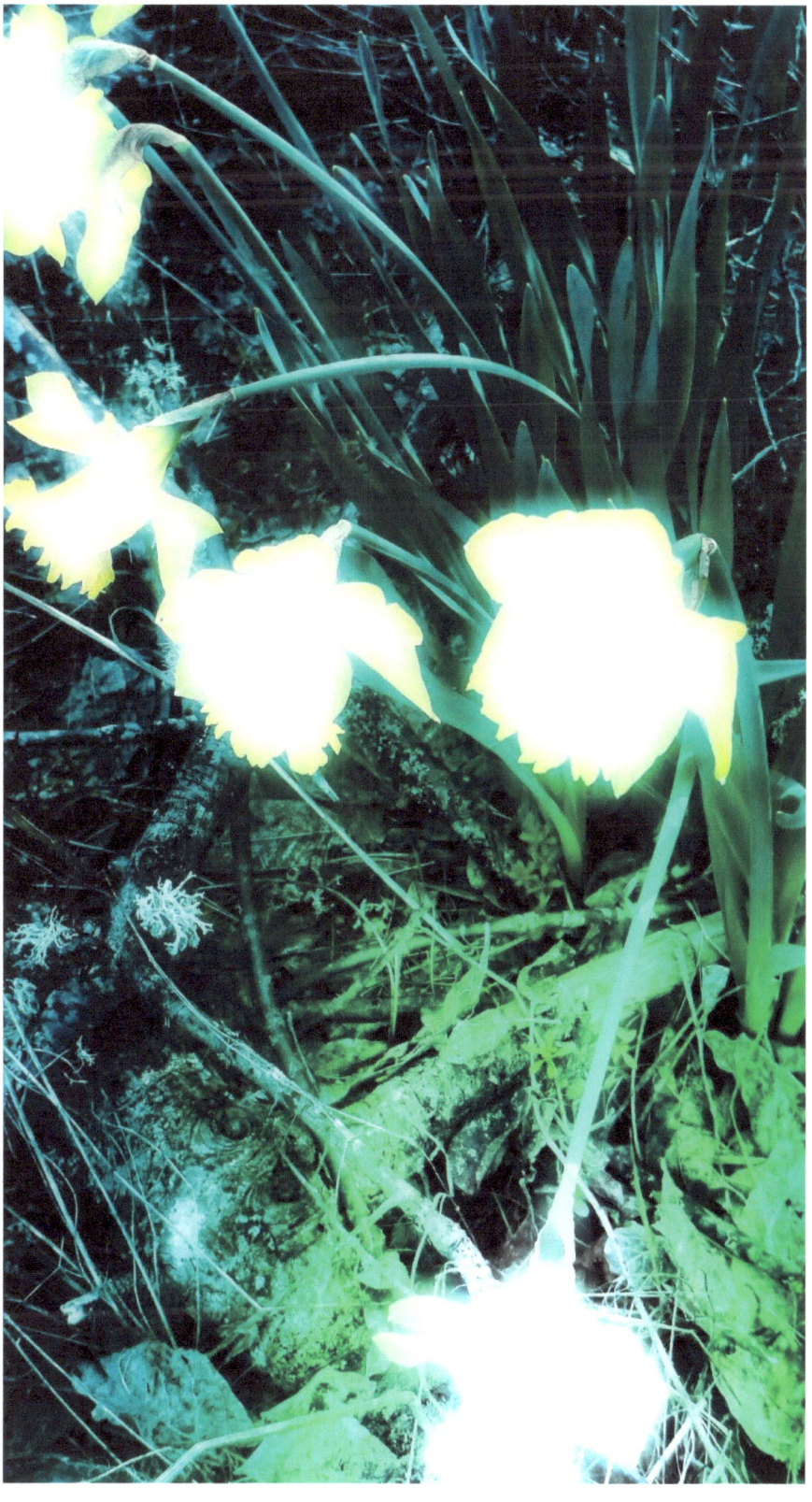

# Deeper Colors

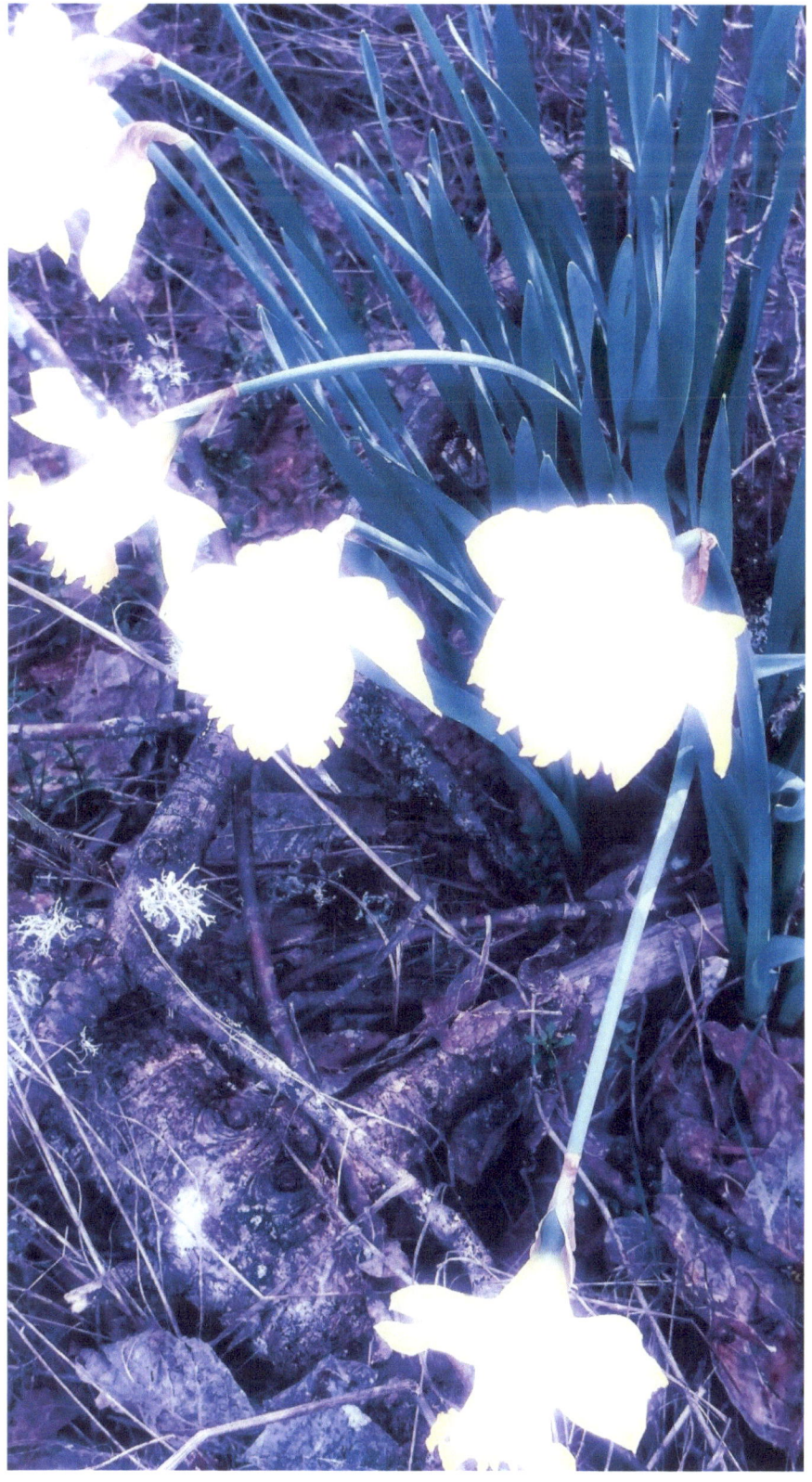

# Branches

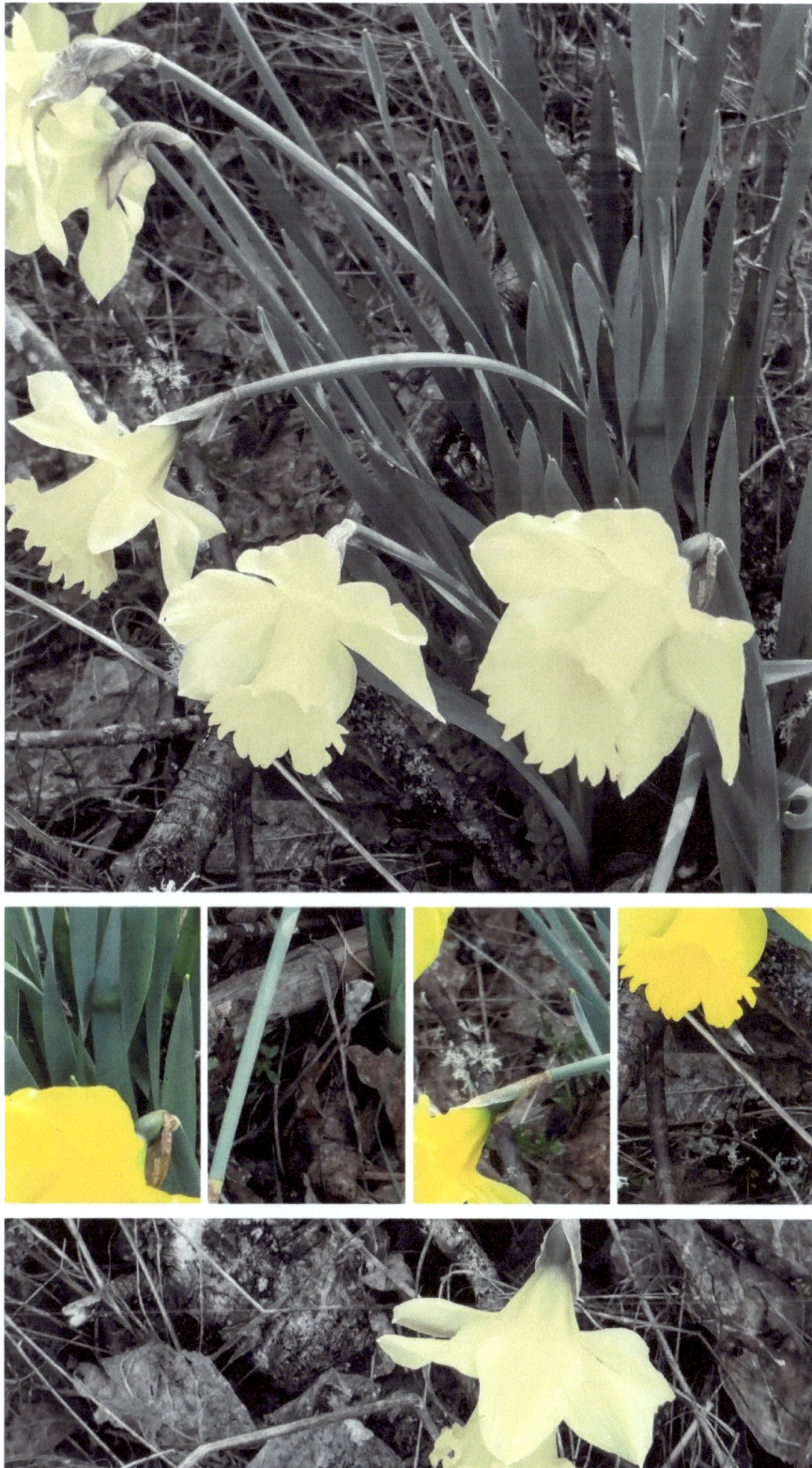

# Red Patina

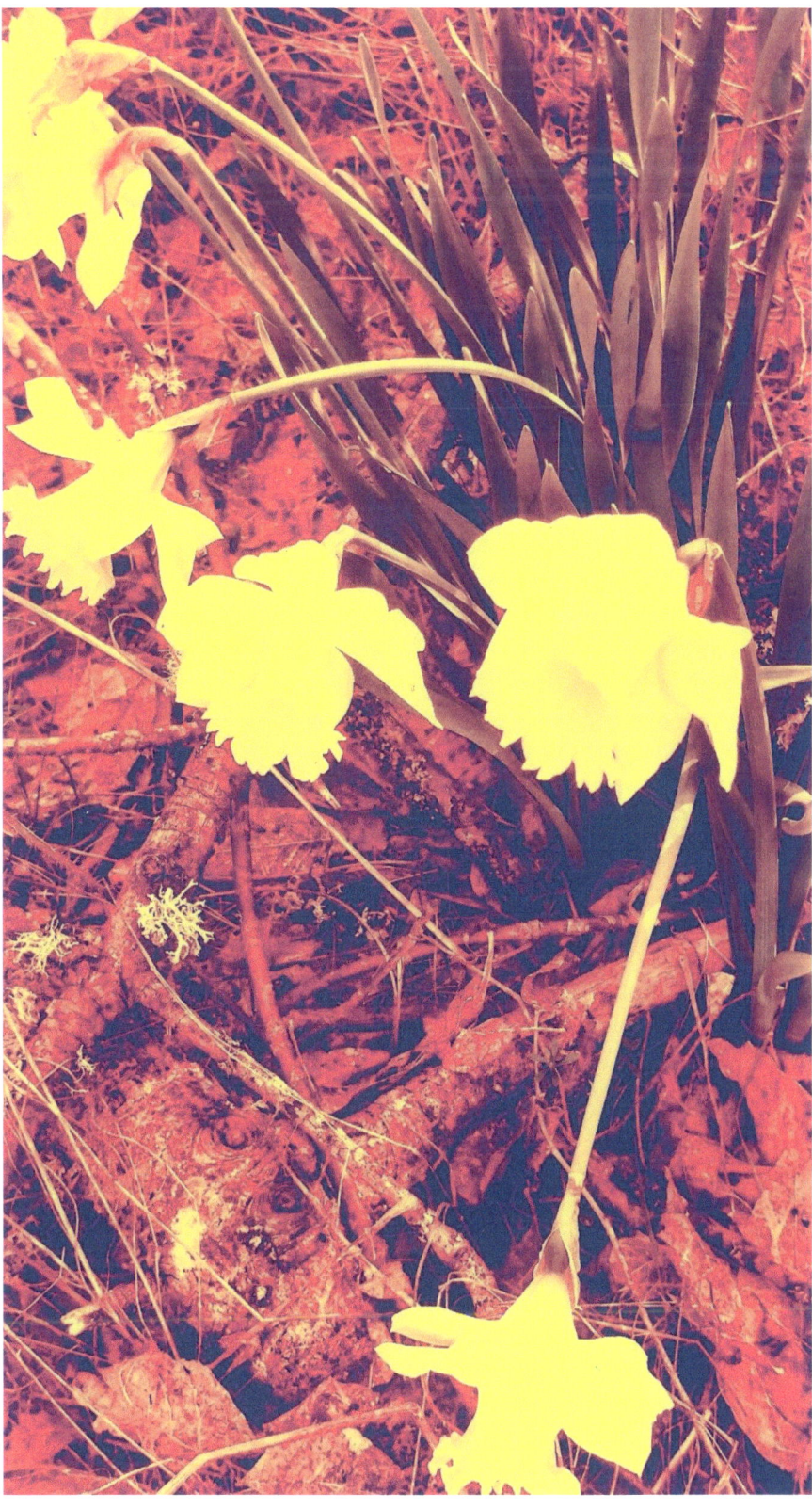

# Fascination

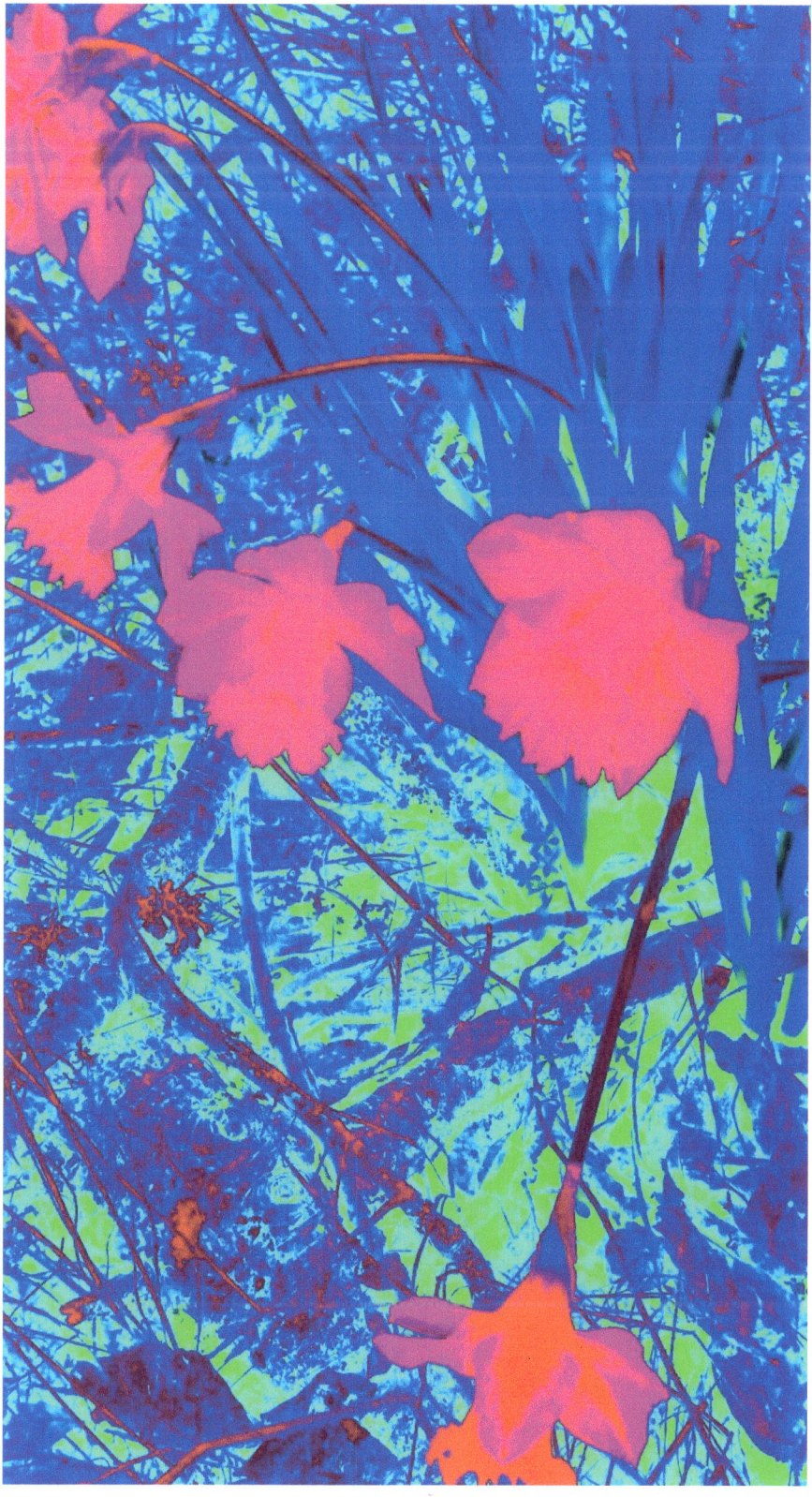

# Subdued

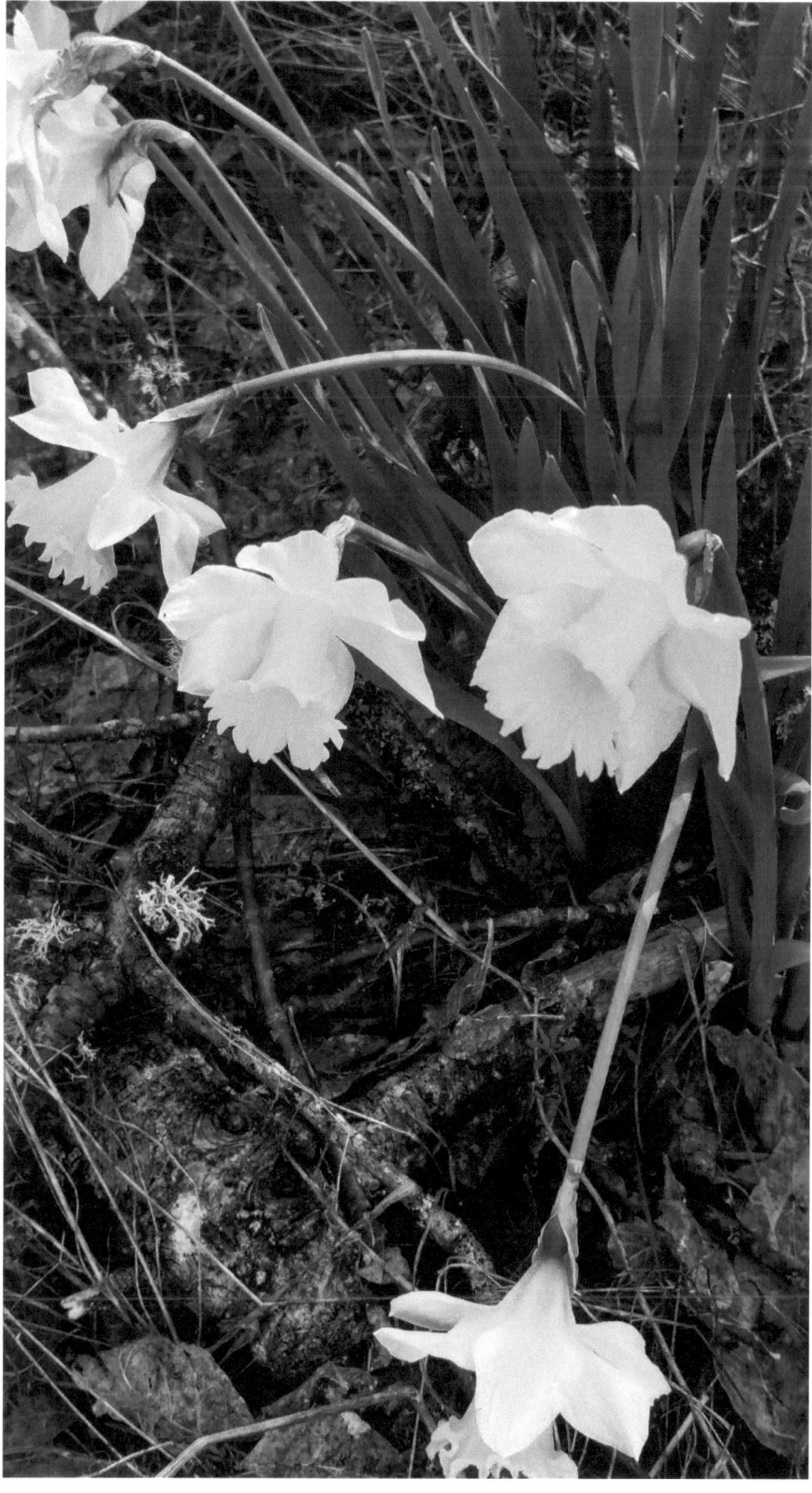

# Futures

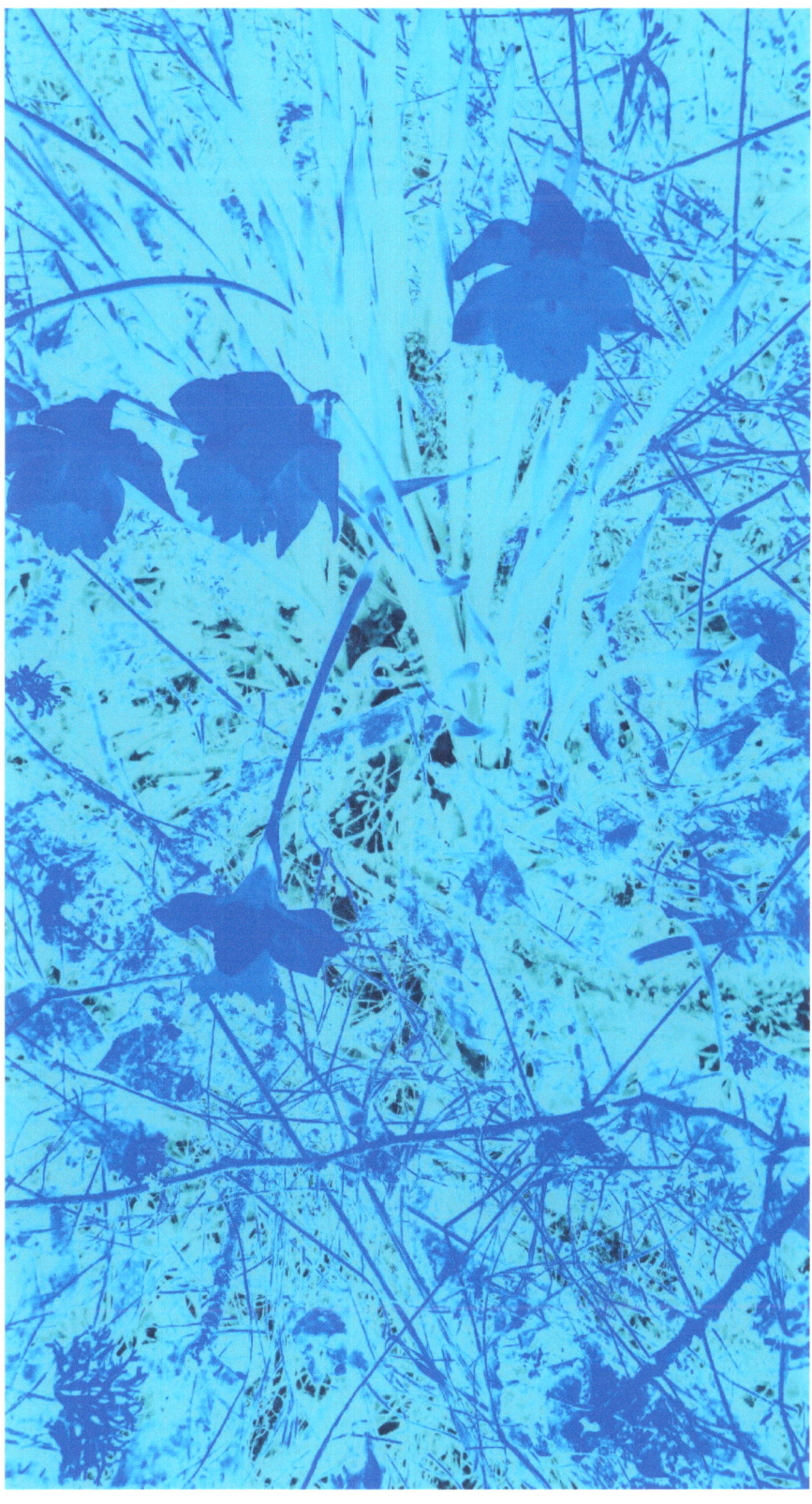

# Partitions

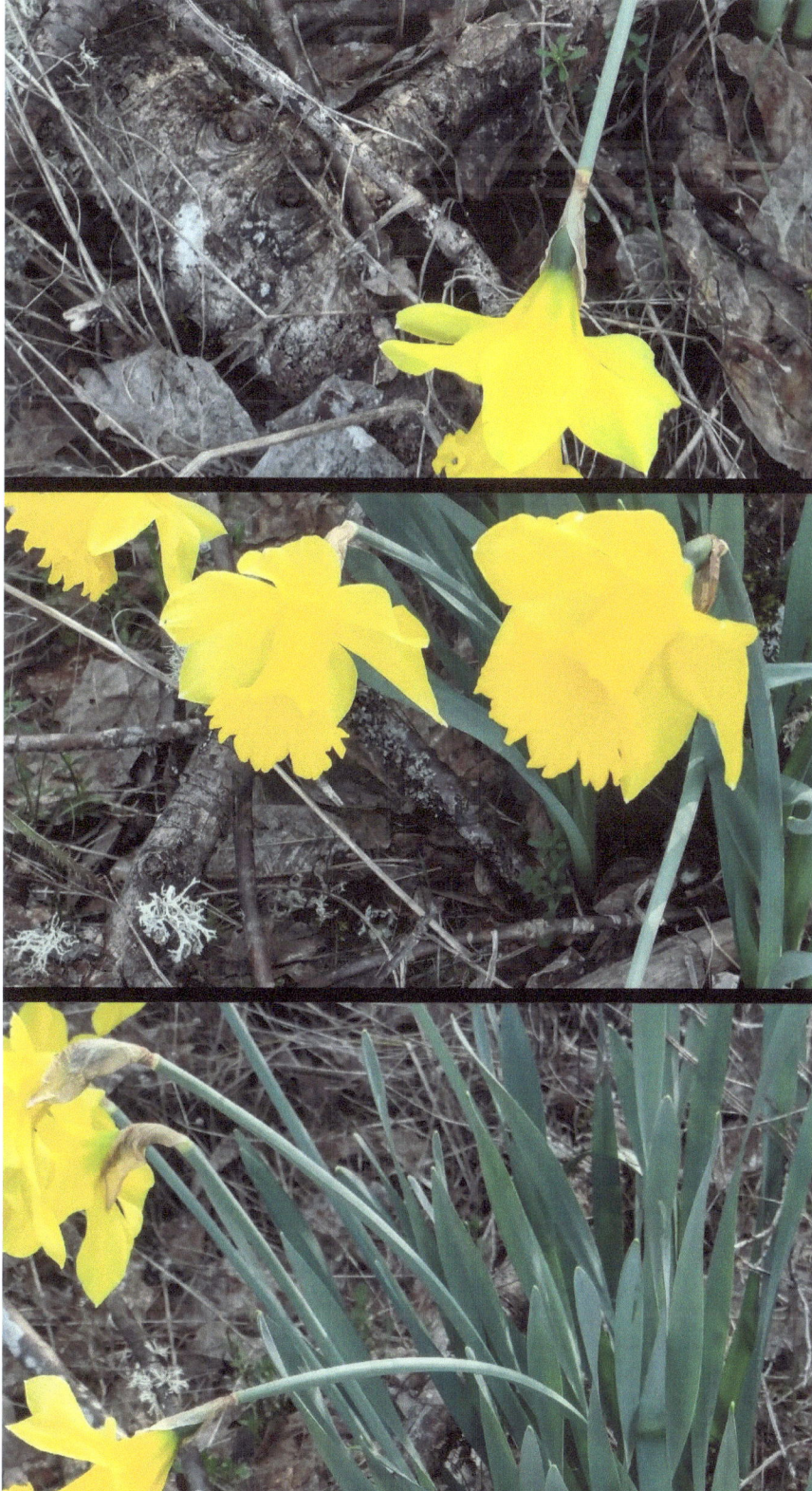

# Remembering

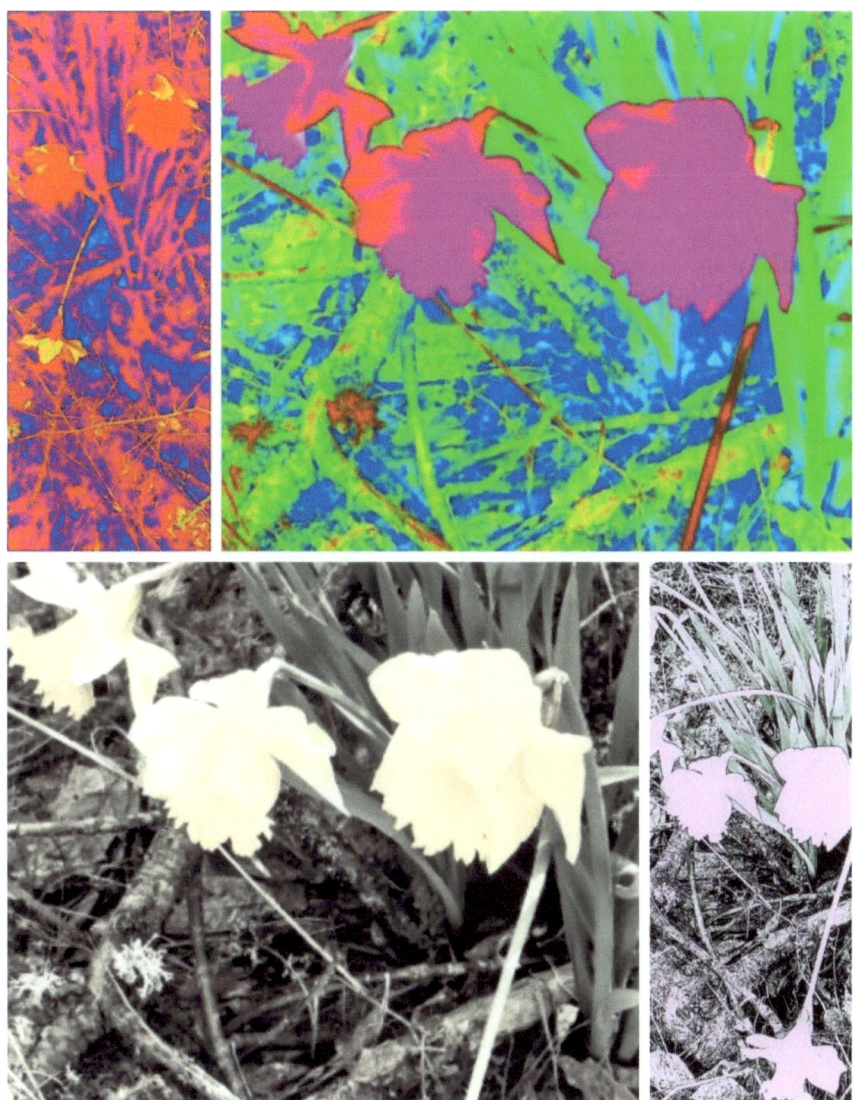